Congratulations! You are holding in your hands one of the most effective tools for test preparation available. The effectiveness of flashcards joined with the convenience and ease of use of a book. We want to offer a quick reminder about how these flashcards are set up and what you can expect.

As you will see, there are two "sets" of flashcards. The top set has a grey background. The bottom set has plain white background. In either case, the question is on the right page and you simply flip the page to see the answer, just like with a traditional flashcard. We highly suggest working through one set at time.

As you will notice, there are different types of questions on the flashcards. None are intended to necessarily be "harder" or "easier", but instead intended to challenge you in different ways. Some have multiple choice questions, which will allow you to think critically as well as get practice for the style of questions you will encounter on the exam. Other flash cards however will provide no clues! This will require you to mentally recall information on your own without the benefit of seeing possible answer choices.

The goal is to engage your brain in different ways so that your studying time is as effective as possible and you retain the necessary information for the test. Unlike with rote memorization or simply reading from a book, you will not experience brain-drain and lose information because you mind is actively engaged the entire time. Less studying, but greater retention of information!

With that, let's get started on the next page. Simply read the question and flip the page to see if you got it right. Remember, work across the entire top (grey) set first, then come back to page 1 and start the bottom (white) set.

Good luck, and again congratulations on your upcoming fantastic test score!

Electrocution dangers exist because a circuit path can be created through any part of the human body through contact to ground. The outcome of an electrocution event is dependent upon the current level, the path through the body that the current follows, and the total amount of time involved. These factors make up what is commonly referred to as what?

    a. The voltage triangulation
    b. The electrocution triangle
    c. Resistance pattern
    d. Path of voltage electrocution

NFPA 70E standards set forth criteria to conduct hazard analyses for working on or near live circuits. The standards require circuit clearing times to be what?

    a. Confirmed through manufacturer data
    b. Twice the discharged voltage
    c. Metered twice and measured once
    d. Split by amperage

**The correct answer is (b.)** The outcome of an electrocution event is dependent upon the current level, the path through the body that the current follows, and the total amount of time involved. These factors make up what is commonly referred to as the electrocution triangle.

**The correct answer is (a.)** NFPA 70E standards set forth criteria to conduct hazard analyses for working on or near live circuits. The standards require circuit clearing times to be confirmed through manufacturer data.

A Confined Space has all three of the following characteristics EXCEPT?

> a. It has limited or restricted means for entry or exit.
>
> b. It has continually supplied air.
>
> c. It is large enough or so configured that an employee can physically enter and perform assigned work.
>
> d. It is not designed for continuous human occupancy.

Which of the following conditions is NOT a descriptor of a hazardous atmosphere?

> a. Has an atmosphere that may expose employees to the risk of death, incapacitation, impairment of ability to self-rescue, injury, or acute illness.
>
> b. Contains a flammable gas, vapor, or mist in excess of 10 percent of its lower flammable limit (LFL).
>
> c. Has an atmospheric oxygen concentration below 19.5 percent or above 23.5 percent.
>
> d. Contains airborne combustible dust at a concentration below its LFL.

**The correct answer is (b.)** A Confined Space has all three of the following characteristics 1) It has limited or restricted means for entry or exit. 2) It is large enough or so configured that an employee can physically enter and perform assigned work. 3) It is not designed for continuous human occupancy. Confined spaces to not have continually supplied air and may be oxygen deficient environments.

**The correct answer is (d.)** All choices are correct descriptors of a Hazardous atmosphere with the exception of d. "Contains airborne combustible dust at a concentration <u>below</u> its LFL." To be correct the statement would read "Airborne combustible dust at a concentration that <u>meets or exceeds</u> its LFL".

A hazard control plan is required under OSHA Standard 29 (CFR) 1910.95 Occupational Noise Exposure where employees are likely to be exposed to noise levels equal to or greater than an 8-hour TWA of _____?

    a. 90 decibels (dB)
    b. 85 decibels (dB)
    c. 65 decibels (dB)
    d. 70 decibels (dB)

A worker responsible for transferring, using, storing, or handing compressed gases should be familiar with the requirements in what standard?

    a. DOT HM-181
    b. NFPA 101
    c. 29 CFR 1910.101
    d. 29 CFR 1926

**The correct answer is (b.)** A hazard control plan is required under OSHA Standard 29 (CFR) 1910.95, Occupational Noise Exposure where employees are likely to be exposed to noise levels equal to or greater than an 8-hour TWA of 85 decibels (dB).

**The correct answer is (c.)** A worker responsible for transferring, using, storing, or handing compressed gases should be familiar with the requirements in 29 CFR 1910.101 Compressed gases (general requirements). DOT HM-181 is Hazardous Materials Training (HM-181) for Shippers, NFPA 101 Life Safety Code, 29 CFR 1926 is Construction Standards.

The permissible exposure limit for asbestos as listed in 29 CFR 1910.1001 is?

    a. 1.0 fibers per cubic centimeter of air (f/cc) / 8 hour day.

    b. 0.1 fibers per cubic centimeter of air (f/cc) / 8 hour day.

    c. 0.5 fibers per cubic centimeter of air (f/cc) / 8 hour day.

    d. 2.0 fibers per cubic centimeter of air (f/cc) / 8 hour day.

Baseline audiometric testing for an employee must be preceded by _____ without workplace noise exposure.

    a. At least 14 hours

    b. At least 16 hours

    c. At least 1 hour

    d. At least 8 hours

**The correct answer is (b.)** The permissible exposure limit for asbestos as listed in 29 CFR 1910.1001 is 0.1 fibers per cubic centimeter of air (f/cc) averaged over an 8 hour day.

**The correct answer is (a.)** Baseline audiometric testing for an employee must be preceded by at least 14 hours without workplace noise exposure.

The OSHA 29 CFR 1910.120 HAZWOPER standard includes training based on a workers function. Which of the following levels of training is <u>not</u> one of the four levels of HAZWOPER?

      a. Hazardous Materials Specialist
      b. First Responder Operations Level
      c. Hazardous Materials Technician
      d. Hazardous Materials Apprentice

Which of the following is the correct formula for a Time Weighted Average (TWA)?

a. $TWA= \dfrac{C_1T_1 + C_2T_2 + C_3 + T_3 .........C_nT_n}{8 \text{ Hours}}$

b. $TWA = C^2T^2 + C_1T_1/8 \text{ Hours}$

c. $TWA = C2T2 + C_1T_1 * 8 \text{ Hours}$

d. $TWA= \dfrac{C_1T_1 + C_2T_2 + C_3 + T_3 .........C_nT_n}{(8 \text{ Hours})^2}$

**The correct answer is (d.)** The OSHA 29 CFR 1910.120 HAZWOPER standard includes training based on a workers function. Hazardous Materials Apprentice level of training is not one of the four levels of HAZWOPER. The levels include Hazardous Materials Awareness Level in addition to Hazardous Materials Specialist, First Responder Operations Level, and Hazardous Materials Technician.

**The correct answer is (a.)** The correct formula for a Time Weighted Average (TWA) is

$$TWA = \frac{C_1T_1 + C_2T_2 + C_3 + T_3 \ldots\ldots C_nT_n}{8 \text{ Hours}}$$

The correct OSHA hazard communication standard label specification for asbestos includes?

    a. Danger - Contains Asbestos Fibers - Cancer and Lung Disease Hazard

    b. Danger - Contains Asbestos Fibers - Peligro - Contiene fibras de asbesto

    c. Danger - Contains Asbestos Fibers - Avoid Creating Dust - Cancer and Lung Disease Hazard

    d. Danger - Cancer and Lung Disease Hazard - Contains Asbestos Fibers

The minimum temperature that a liquid gives off a vapor in a concentration which is concentrated enough to form an ignitable mixture is called what?

    a. The flammable limit

    b. The flash point

    c. Vaporization point

    d. Ignition point

**The correct answer is (c.)** The correct OSHA hazard communication standard label specification for asbestos includes Danger - Contains Asbestos Fibers - Avoid Creating Dust - Cancer and Lung Disease Hazard.

**The correct answer is (b.)** The minimum temperature that a liquid gives off a vapor in a concentration which is concentrated enough to form an ignitable mixture is called the flash point.

The maximum length a single ladder or single section of a ladder may be is _____?

    a. Not to exceed 30 feet

    b. Not to exceed 24 feet

    c. Not to exceed 12 feet

    d. 60 feet

Monitoring for heat and/or cold temperatures requires procedures specific to the extreme measured and may include all of the following EXCEPT:

    a. For heat, the WBGT (Wet Bulb Globe Test).

    b. For cold, measure air temperature, wind and air velocity, and equivalent chill temperature.

    c. For personal monitoring, check heart rate, recovery heart rate, oral temperature, or extent of body water loss.

d. For cold, the WBGT (Wet Bulb Globe Test).

**The correct answer is (a.)** The maximum length a single ladder or single section of a ladder may be is not to exceed 30 feet.

**The correct answer is (d.)** Monitoring for heat and/or cold temperatures requires procedures specific to the extreme measured and may include all of the following EXCEPT: For cold, the WBGT (Wet Bulb Globe Test). This test is used for warm temperatures.

Flammable and combustible liquids stored outside of an outside storage area are required to what?

    a. Be surrounded by a curb at least 6 inches high.

    b. Be in plastic containers

    c. Be labeled by owner

    d. Be ventilated

The acronym NTP stands for normal temperature and pressure which are?

    a. $72^\circ$ F and 15.696 psia

    b. $68^\circ$ F and 13.848 psia

    c. $70^\circ$ F and 13.848 psia

    d. $70^\circ$ F and 14.696 psia

**The correct answer is (a.)** Flammable and combustible liquids stored outside of an outside storage area are required to be surrounded by a curb at least 6 inches high.

**The correct answer is (d.)** The acronym NTP stands for normal temperature and pressure which are $70^\circ$ F and 14.696 pounds per square inch absolute (psia).

How is a loss ratio calculated?

    a. Dividing losses by the number of premiums.

    b. Dividing lost workdays by total work days.

    c. Dividing the total number of injuries multiplied by 200,000.

    d. Dividing the number of accidents by the number of injuries.

29 CFR 1910 subpart 1904.6 is the standard for record keeping. What is the requirement for retention for documents such as the OSHA 200 log?

    a. 30 years following the end of the year to which they relate.

    b. 1 year following the end of the year to which they relate.

    c. 90 days following the end of the year to which they relate.

    d. 5 years following the end of the year to which they relate.

**The correct answer is (a.)** Loss ratio is calculated by dividing losses by the number of premiums.

**The correct answer is (d.)** 29 CFR 1910 subpart 1904.6 is the standard for record keeping. The requirement for retention for documents such as the OSHA 200 log is 5 years following the end of the year to which they relate.

When the ASP is performing fire safety planning which one of the following choices is Not a main objective in planning for fire safety in buildings?

    a. Minimizing property loss for structures and their content.

    b. Maintaining business continuity and minimizing interruption to operations.

    c. Getting building occupants out safely.

    d. Documentation of building material flammability reports.

Indoor Air Quality issues can be mitigated by three basic strategies. Which of the following is not an IAQ mitigation strategy?

    a. Vapor Barrier

    b. Source Control

    c. Ventilation

    d. Air Cleaners

**The correct answer is (d.)** When the ASP is performing fire safety planning, documentation of building material flammability reports is not a main objective in planning for fire safety in buildings. Minimizing property loss for structures and their content, maintaining business continuity and minimizing interruption to operations, and getting building occupants out safely are planning objectives are considered.

**The correct answer is (a.)** Indoor Air Quality issues can be mitigated by three basic strategies. A vapor barrier is not an IAQ mitigation strategy.

A reaction that takes place at a rate which large amounts of energy are released is called?

    a. Oxidation

    b. Polymerization

    c. Opacity

    d. Reactivity

A cutoff wheel with a diameter between 12 to 23 inches can cut a material with a maximum thickness of _____?

    a. 3/16 inch

    b. 1/4 inch

    c. 3/8 inch

    d. 1/2 inch

**The correct answer is (b.)** A reaction that takes place at a rate which large amounts of energy are released is called polymerization.

**The correct answer is (c.)** A cutoff wheel with a diameter between 12 to 23 inches can cut a material with a maximum thickness of 3/8 inches.

Which asbestos hazard class poses the greatest risk to workers and involves the removal of surface materials?

    a. Class I

    b. Class II

    c. Class III

    d. Class IV

Which project management tool do safety management professionals utilize to show project schedule development?

    a. Gantt Chart

    b. UCL/LCL Chart

    c. Pareto Chart

    d. Poisson Chart

**The correct answer is (a.)** Class I poses the greatest risk to workers and involves the removal of surface materials. Basic precautions include establishing regulated areas, daily monitoring, and providing 4 day abatement worker training.

**The correct answer is (a.)** Safety management professionals utilize the Gantt chart project management tool to show project schedule development.

An Associate Safety Professional determines an employee's exposure to a chemical has reached the Action Level (AL). What level have they met?

      a. Fifty percent of the occupational exposure limit (OEL)

      b. Twenty five percent of the occupational exposure limit (OEL)

      c. Fifteen percent of the occupational exposure limit (OEL)

      d. Five percent of the occupational exposure limit (OEL)

The Associate Safety Professional is required to train employees on the OSHA hazard communication standard at what intervals?

      a. On an annual basis

      b. Upon initial assignment to a work area

      c. When a new hazardous material is introduced into the workplace.

      d. Both b and c

**The correct answer is (a.)** An ASP determines an employee's exposure to a chemical has reached the Action Level (AL). They have met fifty percent of the occupational exposure limit (OEL)

**The correct answer is (d.)** The Associate Safety Professional is required to train employees on the OSHA hazard communication standard upon initial assignment to a work area and when a new hazardous material is introduced into the workplace.

Which of the following formulas is used to calculate parts per million ppm?

a.     $\dfrac{\text{parts of contaminant}}{\text{million parts of air}}$

b.     $\dfrac{\text{Volume of contaminant x } 10^6}{\text{total volume}}$

c.     $\dfrac{\text{parts of contaminant}}{\text{million parts of air}}$

d.     $\dfrac{\text{million part air x Vol. contaminant}}{2}$

OSHA requires eyewashes and showers where "the eyes or body of any person may be exposed to injurious corrosive materials, suitable facilities for quick drenching or flushing of the eyes and body shall be provided within the work area for immediate emergency use." Eyewashes/showers should be located?

    a. Within containment.

    b. Within arm's reach of the hazard.

    c. Within 10 seconds walking distance from the hazard.

    d. At the source of the hazard.

**The correct answer is (c.)** The formulas below are both used to calculate parts per million ppm.

c.

$$PPM= \frac{\text{parts of contaminant}}{\text{million parts of air}}$$

and

$$PPM= \frac{\text{Volume of contaminant} \times 10^6}{\text{total volume}}$$

**The correct answer is (c.)** OSHA requires eyewashes and showers where "the eyes or body of any person may be exposed to injurious corrosive materials, suitable facilities for quick drenching or flushing of the eyes and body shall be provided within the work area for immediate emergency use." Eyewashes/showers should be located within 10 seconds walking distance from the hazard.

When the energy-isolating device cannot be locked out, the employer must use tagout. When using tagout, training is required for all employees on the limitations of the tags. Where tagout devices are used they must meet all of the following requirements EXCEPT:

a. MUST clearly identify the employee who applied them and the date that the tag was applied.
b. Be in bilingual format
c. Standardized according to color, shape or size
d. Substantial enough to prevent easy or accidental removal.

Which type of fire detector would be most appropriate for a manufacturing facility that builds wooden shipping crates?
    a. Heat detector
    b. UV flame detection
    c. Photoelectric detector
    d. Smoke analyzing detector

**The correct answer is (b.)** When the energy-isolating device cannot be locked out, the employer must use tagout. When using tagout, training is required for all employees on the limitations of the tags. Where tagout devices are used they must meet all of the following requirements EXCEPT: In bilingual format. They must clearly identify the employee who applied them and the date that the tag was applied, be standardized according to color, shape or size and substantial enough to prevent easy or accidental removal.

**The correct answer is (a.)** A heat detector would be most appropriate fire detector for a manufacturing facility that builds wooden shipping crates. Due to the source material and temperature of the fire.

The Associate Safety Professional will evaluate risks to compare accident data and loss costs. Which of the following choices is not a variable the ASP would evaluate for risk?

a. Accident frequency and loss costs as a function of physical exposure and financial considerations.

b. Physical exposures in terms of property square footage, personnel numbers, and labor hours.

c. Training frequency

d. Payroll and gross revenue financial considerations.

Standards for safety glasses are set by which of the following organizations?

a. American Society for Safety Engineers (ASSE)

b. American Society for Testing and Materials (ASTM)

c. Personal Protective Equipment Standards (PPES)

d. American National Standards Institute (ANSI)

**The correct answer is (c.)** The Associate Safety Professional will evaluate risks to compare accident data and loss costs. Training frequency is not a variable the ASP would evaluate for risk when comparing accident data and loss costs. Accident frequency and loss costs as a function of physical exposure and financial considerations. Physical exposures in terms of property square footage, personnel numbers, and labor hours and payroll and gross revenue financial considerations would be considered.

**The correct answer is (d.)** Standards for safety glasses are set by the American National Standards Institute (ANSI).

When computing the safety life cycle costs, which of the following components is not included?

    a. The analysis phase to identify and estimate potential hazards and risks.

    b. Evaluation if the risk is tolerable within industry or regulatory standards.

    c. Documenting the risk decision into the safety requirements.

    d. Authoring safety life cycle costs policy.

Which of the following accident causal factors would improper job procedures fall?

    a. Worker job practices

    b. Poor supervision

    c. Unsafe conditions

    d. Unsafe materials, tools, or equipment.

**The correct answer is (d.)** When computing the safety life cycle costs authoring safety life cycle costs policy is not included. The analysis, evaluation, and documentation phases are included.

**The correct answer is (b.)** Improper job procedures would fall under poor supervision category of accident causal factor.

Which of the following is NOT included in the procedures the ASP is required to have in place for use of respirators?

    a. Protection in Immediately Dangerous to Life or Health (IDLH) atmospheres

    b. Protection during structural fires

    c. Proper face piece seal protection

    d. Vendor sampling

The process of equalizing the charge between a hazardous waste drum and a transfer container is called?

    a. Stabilization

    b. Grounding

    c. Bonding

    d. Radiant Tapping

**The correct answer is (d.)** Vendor sampling is NOT included in the procedures the ASP is required to have in place for use of respirators. Protection in Immediately Dangerous to Life or Health (IDLH) atmospheres, protection during structural fires, and proper face piece seal protection are required implementation procedures.

**The correct answer is (b.)** The process of equalizing the charge between a hazardous waste drum and a transfer container is called grounding.

The Associate Safety Professional can best identify hazards in the workplace through?

      a. Review of safety and industry journals.

      b. Analysis of prior year accident and injury trends.

      c. Conducting comprehensive worksite analysis

      d. Conducting comprehensive safety standard reviews.


Which type of OSHA violation will result in a fine of up to $250,000 if an employee death occurs?

      a. Failure to abate

      b. Serious violation

      c. Willful violation

      d. Repeat violation

**The correct answer is (c.)** The Associate Safety Professional can best identify hazards in the workplace through conducting a comprehensive worksite analysis.

**The correct answer is (c.)** A willful violation will result in a fine of up to $250,000 if an employee death occurs upon criminal conviction.

The Associate Safety Professional must post the OSHA 200 log by _____ and must remain posted until _____ of each year.

    a. January 1, March 1
    b. January 1, June 1
    c. February 1, March 1
    d. February 1, June 1

The Resource Conservation and Recovery Act (RCRA) created a cradle to grave management system of current and future wastes. RCRA requirements require facilities that generate wastes to do all of the following EXCEPT?

    a. Identify and label all wastes
    b. Quantify green financial environment initiatives
    c. Maintain records and train waste handlers
    d. Use permitted waste treatment and disposal facilities

**The correct answer is (c.)** The Associate Safety Professional must post the OSHA 200 log by February 1, and must remain posted until March 1, of each year.

**The correct answer is (b.)** The Resource Conservation and Recovery Act (RCRA) created a cradle to grave management system of current and future wastes. RCRA requirements require facilities that generate wastes to do all of the following EXCEPT quantify green financial environment initiatives.

The waste generator classification for the conditionally exempt category is categorized by what level of waste?

      a. Less than 100 kg/month and no more than 1kg of acutely hazardous waste

      b. 100 to 1000 kg/month

      c. A minimum of 100 kg/month and no more than 1kg of acutely hazardous waste

      d. Over 1000 kg/month

A safety professional is designing a class on ergonomic safety. As they prepare presentation slides they have reviewed the slides to ensure they have included the three learning domains. Which of the following is not one of the learning domains?

      a. Cognitive

      b. Affective

      c. Psychomotor

      d. Stochastic

**The correct answer is (a.)** The waste generator classification for the conditionally exempt category is categorized by less than 100 kg/month and no more than 1kg of acutely hazardous waste.

**The correct answer is (d.)** A safety professional is designing a class on ergonomic safety. As they prepare presentation slides they have reviewed the slides to ensure they have included the three learning domains. Stochastic is not one of the learning domains. The three domains are <u>cognitive</u> relating to the thought process, <u>affective</u> relating to an external expression of emotion associated with an idea or action, and <u>psychomotor</u> relating to bodily movement triggered by mental activity, especially voluntary muscle action.

A safety professional was performing research on safety accidents related to scaffold workers. They wanted to know if their accident data for their employees is similar or different to the general injury statistics for scaffolding accidents. They are only testing the sampling mean. What statistical test would they use?

        a. one-sample Z test

        b. One-way ANOVA

        c. Chi-square

        d. Pearson correlation

A confidence interval is a type of interval estimate of a population parameter used to indicate the reliability of an estimate. A 95% confidence interval reflects a significance level of what?

        a. 0.025

        b. 0.05

        c. 0.101

        d. 0.125

**The correct answer is (a.)** If a safety professional was performing research on safety accidents related to scaffold workers and they wanted to know if their accident data for their employees is similar or different to the general injury statistics for scaffolding accidents and they are only testing the sampling mean. They would use a one-sample Z test because it is only used for the sampling mean and test they hypothesis to know whether the average of the sample suggests that the workers come from a population with a known mean or whether it comes from a different population.

**The correct answer is (b.)** A confidence interval is a type of interval estimate of a population parameter used to indicate the reliability of an estimate. A 95% confidence interval reflects a significance level 0.05.

Which data sets are required to calculate the upper and lower control limit?

      a. The median and mode.

      b. The standard deviation and sum of the high and low extreme.

      c. The mean and standard deviations of your data set.

      d. Square root of the high and low measures.

If a safety professional were trying to find the length of c below and a=10 feet and b=20 feet, c would equal what?

**TRIGONOMETRIC FUNCTIONS**

$\sin A = a/c$      $\cos A = b/c$      $\tan A = a/b$

$c^2 = a^2 + b^2 - 2ab \cos C$

$$\frac{a}{\sin A} = \frac{b}{\sin B} = \frac{c}{\sin C}$$

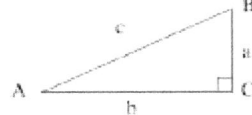

      a. 30.00 feet

      b. 22.36 feet

      c. 25.54 feet

      d. 27.98 feet

**The correct answer is (c.)** The mean and standard deviations of your data set are required to calculate the upper and lower control limit.

**The correct answer is (b.)** The BSCP provides an examination reference guide for the ASP. Using the guide and trigonometric function in the chart, if a safety professional were trying to find the length of c below and a=10 feet and b=20 feet, c would equal 22.36 feet.

Understanding learning skills of students for safety training purposes requires the safety professional differentiate between education and training. Which of the following statements below is correct concerning education and training?

    a. Education requires a minimum of 40 hours of didactic classroom time.

    b. Education focuses on how to do something.

    c. B and d are correct.

    d. Training focuses on developing skills or behavior change.

Poisson distribution applies when you are counting the number of objects in a certain volume or the number of events in a certain time period. If a safety professional knows the average number of counts and wants to know the chance of actually observing various numbers of occurrences or events i.e. accidents they can calculate the Poisson probability. If a company has on average 30 accidents per month what would the cumulative probability of occurrence over 30 days be?

    a. less than 50%

    b. greater than 50%

    c. equal to 50%

    d. 100%

**The correct answer is (c.)** Understanding learning skills of students for safety training purposes requires the safety professional differentiate between education and training. Education focuses on how to do something and training focuses on developing skills or behavior change.

**The correct answer is (b.)** If a safety professional knows the average number of counts and wants to know the chance of actually observing various numbers of occurrences or events i.e. accidents they can calculate the Poisson probability. If a company has on average 30 accidents per month the cumulative probability of occurrence over 30 days will be greater than 50%. Based on 30 events the exact probability would be 7.263% and the cumulative probability would be 54.835%

A safety professional is training supervisors and management personnel to prevent workplace violence. All of the following are prevention tips EXCEPT?

    a. Proactively hire and fire employees to reduce violent behavior.

    b. Educate employees on ways to improve communication and relationships.

    c. Recognize and deal with threats and violent behavior.

    d. Minimize violent situations so they will not be in the forefront of employees thoughts.

Which risk management strategy is categorized by buying insurance?

    a. Transference

    b. Mitigation

    c. Contingencies

    d. Avoidance

**The correct answer is (d.)** A safety professional is training supervisors and management personnel to prevent workplace violence. Minimizing violent situations so they will not be in the forefront of employees thoughts is not a proactive measure and will lead to poor management of the violence in the workplace program and loss of employee safety perception.

**The correct answer is (a.)** The transference risk management strategy is characterized by buying insurance and transferring risk to another party. Avoidance is characterized by completely avoiding the risk. Mitigation is characterized by changing a plan to reduce risk.
Contingencies are characterized by developing alternate plans in the even a risk event occurs

When performing safety calculations, which physical constant is represented by the calculation $32.2 \text{ ft/sec}^2 = 9.8 \text{ m/sec}^2$?

    a. Velocity of light

    b. Acceleration of gravity

    c. Planck's constant

    d. Avagadro's number

The NIOSH lifting index provides a relative estimate of the physical stress associated with a manual lifting job. Which of the formulas below represents the Lifting Index (LI)?

a. $LI = \dfrac{\text{Load Weight}}{\text{Recommended Load Weight}}$

b. $LI = \dfrac{\text{Load Weight}}{\text{Potential Load Weight}}$

c. $LI = \dfrac{\text{Potential Load Weight}}{\text{Recommended Load Weight}}$

d. $LI = \dfrac{\text{Load Max Weight}}{\text{Potential Max Load Weight}}$

**The correct answer is (b.) When performing safety calculations, acceleration of gravity is represented by the calculation 32.2 ft/sec$^2$ = 9.8 m/sec$^2$.**

PHYSICAL CONSTANTS

acceleration of gravity = 32.2 ft/sec$^2$ = 9.8 m/sec$^2$

velocity of light = 3.0 x 10$^8$ m/sec

Planck's constant = 6.626 x 10$^{-34}$ J-sec

Avagadro's number = 6.024 x 10$^{23}$/ gram-mole

**The correct answer is (a.)** The NIOSH lifting index provides a relative estimate of the physical stress associated with a manual lifting job. A.represents the Lifting Index (LI)?

a. LI=        $\dfrac{\text{Load Weight}}{\text{Recommended Load Weight}}$

When developing a system safety review an ASP is determining probability of occurrence for an event. Conditional probability is the probability of some event such as event (A) given the occurrence of some other event (B). Which formula can be used to derive conditional probability?

    a. $P(A \mid B) = P(A \cap B)$
    b. $P(A \mid B) = P(A \cap B)/P(B)$
    c. $P(A \mid B) = P(A \cap B)^2$
    d. $P(A \mid B) = \dfrac{P(A \cap B)}{P(B)}$

The EPA has established characteristics for hazardous waste classification. Which of the following is not a property assigned a series waste code?

    a. Ignitability
    b. Corrosivity
    c. Reactivity
    d. Teratogenicity

**The correct answer is (b.)** Conditional probability is the probability of some event such as event (A) given the occurrence of some other event (B). P(A | B) = P(A n B)/P(B) can be used to derive conditional probability.

**The correct answer is (d.)** The EPA has established characteristics for hazardous waste classification. Teratogenicity is not a property assigned a series waste code. The four properties are Ignitability, Corrosivity, Reactivity, and toxicity.

The shipping of hazardous wastes requires all of the following EXCEPT?

    a. Packages and vehicles must be properly labeled, marked, and placarded.

    b. Highway shippers need the appropriate license endorsements.

    c. Shippers must be listed under the DOT registration program.

    d. Vehicles used in transport must be limited to 23000 lbs gvw.


In ergonomic studies the recommended weight limit (RWL) can be used to assist in ergonomic design. Which of the following is not a use for calculations of the RWL or a lifting index?

    a. The lifting index can be used to estimate the relative magnitude of physical stress for a task or job.

    b. The LI can be used to prioritize and rank ergonomic hazards.

    c. The recommended weight limit can be used to calculate individual stressor multipliers.

    d. The LI can be used to perform an ergonomic evaluation.

**The correct answer is (d.)** The shipping of hazardous wastes requires all of the following EXCEPT vehicles used in transport must be limited to 23000 lbs gvw. Packages and vehicles must be properly labeled, marked, and placarded. Highway shippers need the appropriate license endorsements. And, shippers must be listed under the DOT registration program.

**The correct answer is (d.)** In ergonomic studies the recommended weight limit (RWL) can be used to assist in ergonomic design. The LI cannot be used to perform an ergonomic evaluation only aid in the measurement.

Personal Protective Equipment to protect against blood borne pathogens and infectious materials requires all of the following EXCEPT?

  a. Taking allergic conditions into consideration.

  b. Provision of PPE at no cost.

  c. PPE may not allow for pass through of material or substances.

  d. PPE requires only coats and gloves.

Physical security management plans require all of the following EXCEPT?

  a. Annual cost evaluation

  b. Annual effectiveness evaluations

  c. Established program procedures

  d. Identification of responsibilities

**The correct answer is (d.)** Personal Protective Equipment to protect against blood borne pathogens and infectious materials requires taking allergic conditions into consideration, provision of PPE at no cost, and PPE may not allow for pass through of material or substances. The EXCEPTION is PPE requires only coats and gloves. This is incorrect as PPE includes clothing, gloves, coats, face shields, eye protection, and respiratory controls at a minimum.

**The correct answer is (a.)** Physical security management plans require all of the following EXCEPT an annual cost evaluation.

Which of the following is not a component of a worksite analysis for workplace violence?

    a. Records Analysis and Tracking
    b. Hazard Control
    c. Employee Screening Survey
    d. Workplace Security Analysis

Protection for occupational exposure to radiation includes all of the following EXCEPT?

    a. Limiting length of exposure
    b. Shielding exposed workers with PPE
    c. Reducing the radioactive strength mechanically.
    d. Increasing distance from the source.

**The correct answer is (b.)** Hazard Control is not a component of a worksite analysis for workplace violence. Hazard Control is used to ensure security hazards are controlled but not a part of the analysis.

**The correct answer is (c.)** Protection for occupational exposure to radiation includes limiting length of exposure, shielding exposed workers with PPE, and increasing distance from the source. Reducing the radioactive strength mechanically is not a method used.

A leading indicator for safety may be a safety intervention which is defined as an attempt to change how things are done in order to improve safety. Which of the following is not considered a safety intervention?

      a. Engineering intervention

      b. Review of accident data

      c. Administrative procedures

      d. Training programs

Which environment would an employee wear a thermoluminescent TLD Badge?

      a. Radiology technician in a hospital

      b. Plant worker for benzene production

      c. Lawn maintenance worker

      d. Press machine operator

**The correct answer is (b.)** A leading indicator for safety may be a safety intervention which is defined as an attempt to change how things are done in order to improve safety. Review of accident data is not considered a safety <u>intervention.</u> Interventions may include engineering intervention, administrative procedures, and training programs.

**The correct answer is (a.)** An employee would wear a thermoluminescent TLD badge if they were a radiology technician in a hospital. A thermoluminescent dosimeter TLD badge is used to determine ionizing radiation received by the wearer.

A safety professional working as a project team leader may employ the use of the terminology used to describe the act of decreasing the duration of a project by adding resources. This action is called what?

      a. Driving
      b. Speeding up
      c. Crashing
      d. Fast tracking

The OSHA Standard for wheel equipment grinders (29 CFR 1910.215) requires grinder adjustable work rests have a maximum of what width from the wheel?

      a. 1/8 inch
      b. 1/4 inch
      c. 3/8 inch
      d. 1/2 inch

**The correct answer is (c.)** A safety professional working as a project team leader may employ the use of the terminology used to describe the act of decreasing the duration of a project by adding resources. This action is called crashing the schedule.

**The correct answer is (a.)** The OSHA Standard for wheel equipment grinders (29 CFR 1910.215) requires grinder adjustable work rests have a maximum 1/8 inch width from the wheel.

OSHA 1910.23, Guarding Floor and Wall
Openings and Holes defines a floor hole as
- a. less than 12 inches but more than 1 inch
- b. less than 3 inches but more than 2 inches
- c. less than 4 inches but more than 1 inch
- d. less than 6 inches but more than 2 inches

OSHA regulations do not specify minimum
operating or installation requirements for
eyewashes. The primary consensus standard used
for eye washes is from?
- a. American Society for Testing and
  Materials (ASTM)
- b. American National Standards Institute
  (ANSI)
- c. American Society for Safety Engineers
  (ASSE)
- d. National Safety Council (NSC)

**The correct answer is (a.)** OSHA 1910.23, Guarding Floor and Wall Openings and Holes defines a floor hole as less than 12 inches but more than 1 inch.

**The correct answer is (b.)** OSHA regulations do not specify minimum operating or installation requirements for eyewashes. The primary consensus standard used for eye washes is from American National Standards Institute (ANSI) Standard Z358.

Audiometric testing requires all of the following documentation EXCEPT?

    a. Name and job classification of the employee.

    b. Date of the Audiogram

    c. Name of supervisor

    d. Date of audiometer calibration

Which of the following air emission standards must a hazardous waste incinerator follow?

    a. Environmental Cleanup Responsibility Act (ECRA)

    b. Air Standards Act

    c. Clean Air Act

    d. Active Emissions Act

**The correct answer is (c.)** Audiometric testing requires all of the following documentation name and job classification of the employee, date of the Audiogram, and date of audiometer calibration, but not the name of supervisor.

**The correct answer is (c.)** A hazardous waste incinerator must follow the Clean Air Act air emission standards.

Eyewear shades used in welding operations for shielded metal arc welding require as recommended by ANSI Z87 a shade number of?

a. Ten
b. Three
c. Four
d. Six

The OSHA requirements for use of compressed air for cleaning are contained in 29 CFR 1910.242(b) require the psi be less than what?

a. 20 psi
b. 40 psi
c. 25 psi
d. 30 psi

**The correct answer is (a.)** Eyewear shades used in welding operations for shielded metal arc welding require as recommended by ANSI Z87 a shade number of ten.

**The correct answer is (d.)** The OSHA requirements for use of compressed air for cleaning are contained in 29 CFR 1910.242(b) require the psi be less than 30.

Material handling and working on loading docks typically requires all of the following personal protective equipment (PPE) EXCEPT?

    a. Eye protection

    b. Steel-toed safety shoes or boots

    c  Hand and forearm protection, such as gloves, for loads with sharp or rough edges.

    d. Respirators

The net present value formula may be needed to determine the costs benefits of undergoing an engineering control. The formula for NPV is

$$PV = \frac{P_t}{(1 + r)^t}$$

Which of the following choices is an incorrect description of the value?

a. r is the current rate

b. Pt is the dollar value of the future amount in time

c. r is the discount rate

d. PV is the present value of the amount invested

**The correct answer is (d.)** Material handling and working on loading docks typically requires all of the following (PPE) eye protection, steel-toed safety shoes or boots personal protective equipment hand and forearm protection, such as gloves, for loads with sharp or rough edges and not respirators.

**The correct answer is (a.)** The net present value formula may be needed to determine the costs benefits of undergoing an engineering control. The incorrect choice is r is the current rate.

Which of the following is NOT an example of an administrative control for MSD hazards?

    a. Employee rotation

    b. Alternative tasks

    c. Employer authorized changes in work pace

    d. Documented mandatory physical conditioning

Abatement certification requires the employer must certify to OSHA that the cited violation has been abated within _____?

    a. 7 calendar days after the abatement date

    b. 10 calendar days after the abatement date

    c. Is not required

    d. 14 calendar days after the abatement date

**The correct answer is (d.)** Documented mandatory physical conditioning would not be an administrative control as mandatory physical conditioning may exacerbate the MSD condition and do not qualify as an administrative or engineering control.

**The correct answer is (b.)** Abatement certification requires the employer must certify to OSHA that the cited violation has been abated within 10 calendar days after the abatement date.

Which of the following is not a requirement of procedures for interior structural firefighting?

 a. All employees engaged in interior structural firefighting use SCBAs.

 b. All employees engaged in interior structural firefighting use PAPRs.

 c. At least two employees are located outside the IDLH atmosphere.

 d. At least two employees enter the IDLH atmosphere and maintain visual and voice contact at all times.

Rubber-insulating gloves for use in live electrical operations operating in excess of 50 volts must be type I and must meet the minimum requirements of American Society for Testing and Materials (ASTM) standard _____.

 a. ASTM D 120-9

 b. ASTM F1505

 c. ASTM D 1048-93

 d. ASTM D 120-87

**The correct answer is (b.)** "All employees engaged in interior structural firefighting use PAPRs" is not a requirement of procedures for interior structural firefighting. Powered air purifying respirators use the ambient air and are not used for structural fires.

**The correct answer is (a.)** Rubber-insulating gloves for use in live electrical operations operating in excess of 50 volts must be type I and must meet the minimum requirements of American Society for Testing and Materials (ASTM) standard ASTM D 120-9 Standard Specification for Rubber Insulating Gloves. The remaining standards are ASTM F1505 Standard Specification for Insulated and Insulating Hand Tools, ASTM D 1048-93 Rubber-Insulating Blankets Test Method, ASTM D 120-87 Rubber-Insulating Gloves Test Methods.

Using ANSI/ASSE A1264.2 American National
Standard titled: "Standard for the Provision of Slip
Resistance on Walking/Working Surfaces" a
coefficient of friction of 1 is?

    a. Neutral
    b. Very slippery
    c. Not slippery at all
    d. Extremely slippery

Compute the mean, median, and mode for the
following numbers 8, 2, 5, 1, 7, 12, 16, 4, 22 then
select the correct choice.

    a. Mode is none Mean is 7.25 Median is 8
    b. Mode is none Mean is 8.56 Median is 7
    c. Mode is 12 Mean is 7 Median is 8
    d. Mode is none Mean is 9 Median is 7.5

**The correct answer is (c.).** Using ANSI/ASSE A1264.2 American National Standard titled: "Standard for the Provision of Slip Resistance on Walking/Working Surfaces" a coefficient of friction of 1 is not slippery at all.

**The correct answer is (b.)** When computing the mean, median, and mode for the following numbers 8, 2, 5, 1, 7, 12, 16, 4, 22. Mode is none, Mean is 8.56, Median is 7.

Under the respiratory fit testing standard 1910.134
a qualitative fit test may only be used to fit test
negative pressure air purifying respirators that must
achieve a fit factor of?

    a. 100 or less
    b. 100 or greater
    c. 150 or less
    d. 200 or less

Posted citations as a result of OSHA standard
violation are required to be posted until the
violation is abated or _____
whichever is later.

    a. For 3 working days
    b. For 7 working days
    c. For 14 working days
    d. For 21 working days

**The correct answer is (a.)** Under the respiratory fit testing standard 1910.134 a qualitative fit test may only be used to fit test negative pressure air purifying respirators that must achieve a fit factor of 100 or less.

**The correct answer is (a.)** Posted citations as a result of OSHA standard violation are required to be posted until the violation is abated or for three working days whichever is later. The filing of a contest does not affect the posting requirement.

The main reason safety management programs fail is?

> a. Organizational emphasis is placed on activity oriented elements.
>
> b. Organization managers ignore basic management techniques
>
> c. Management fails to clearly define goals.
>
> d. a and b

What is the standard deviation of the following dataset of monthly injuries: 14, 17, 29, 34, 21?

> a. 9.42
>
> b. 8.33
>
> c. 3.43
>
> d. 5.82

**The correct answer is (d.)** The main reason safety management programs fail is that organizational emphasis is placed on activity oriented elements and organization managers ignore basic management techniques.

**The correct answer is (b.)** The standard deviation of the following dataset of monthly injuries: 14, 17, 29, 34, 21 is 8.33.

Which of the following terms describes the maximum allowed OSHA exposure for workers during an 8 hour workday or 40 hour workweek?

      a. Exposure limit
      b. Ceiling limit
      c. Short term exposure limit (STEL)
      d. Permissible exposure limit (PEL)

A black cartridge on a respirator would protect against?

      a. Acid gas
      b. Organic Vapors
      c. Radioactive Material
      d. Dust and Mists

**The correct answer is (d)** The term which describes the maximum allowed OSHA exposure for workers during an 8 hour workday or 40 hour workweek is Permissible exposure limit (PEL). The Short term exposure limit (STEL) is the 15-min time weighted average exposure that should not be exceeded at any time during a workday even if the 8 hour time weighted average is within the threshold limit value. The Ceiling limit is the absolute exposure limit that should not be exceeded at any time.

**The correct answer is (b)** A black cartridge on a respirator would protect against organic vapors. Acid gas cartridges are white, radioactive material cartridges are purple and dust and mists are orange.

Compressed gas cylinders should never be exposed
to temperatures greater than?

    a. 200 degrees Fahrenheit
    b. 125 degrees Fahrenheit
    c. 100 degrees Fahrenheit
    d. 150 degrees Fahrenheit

Class A fire protection and extinguishing systems
must have a travel distance of no more than
_____ feet?

    a. 75
    b. 100
    c. 25
    d. 50

**The correct answer is (b)** Compressed gas cylinders should never be exposed to temperatures greater than 125 degrees Fahrenheit.

**The correct answer is (a)** Class A fire protection and extinguishing systems must have a travel distance of no more than 75 feet.

To be classified as flammable a liquid must have a flashpoint which is:

    a. above 200 degrees Fahrenheit
    b. below 200 degrees Fahrenheit
    c. above 100 degrees Fahrenheit
    d. below 100 degrees Fahrenheit

Live parts of electrical equipment which operates at _____ volts or higher must be guarded against accidental contact.

    a. 100
    b. 120
    c. 24
    d. 50

**The correct answer is (d)** To be classified as flammable a liquid must have a flashpoint which below 100 degrees Fahrenheit.

**The correct answer is (d)** Live parts of electrical equipment which operates at 50 volts or higher must be guarded against accidental contact.

A local chemical effect refers to an adverse health effect that takes place at the point or area of contact caused by what?

    a. a chemical that injures the skin, eyes, or respiratory system

    b. repeated exposure to a chemical

    c. a single exposure to a chemical

    d. only teratogenic compounds

Displaying accident rate data to organizational management is best reflected by the use of what diagram?

    a. Cause and effect Ishikawa diagram

    b. Process flow diagram

    c. Histogram

    d. Failure modes and effects analysis (FMEA)

**The correct answer is (a)** A local chemical effect refers to an adverse health effect that takes place at the point or area of contact caused by what a chemical that injures the skin, eyes, or respiratory system.

**The correct answer is (c)** Displaying accident rate data to organizational management is best reflected by the use of a histogram displayed by accident category or trend.

Project management methods to determine risk management strategies requires a quantitative analysis of impact and probability. The formula for a quantitative analysis of probability, impact and expected value is?

     a. EV=P x I
     b. PI = 2EV
     c. EV=2prv
     d. 2r – 3EV = P

Which is the correct definition of expected value?

     a. Frequency times impact of risk.
     b. Probability times impact of a risk.
     c. Rate of return based on change.
     d. Value based on change.

**The correct answer is (a)** Project management methods to determine risk management strategies requires a quantitative analysis of impact and probability. The formula for a quantitative analysis of probability, impact and expected value is EV=P x I. The remaining answers were fabricated.

**The correct answer is (b)** The correct definition of expected value is probability times impact of a risk.

Which of the following instructional techniques is most effective for decontamination training?

        a. Demonstration hands on technique

        b. Information sheet

        c. Visual aid

        d. quiz

General Industry Standards 1910 require a guardrail be at minimum _____ inches to protect the greatest number of people from falling?

        a. 32 inches

        b. 36 inches

        c. 40 inches

        d. 42 inches

**The correct answer is (a)** Demonstration hands on instructional technique is most effective for decontamination training.

**The correct answer is (d)** General Industry Standards 1910 require a guardrail be at minimum 42 inches to protect the greatest number of people from falling.

A commonly reported problem associated with tingling, pain, or numbness in the thumb and first three fingers is referred to as:

      a. Asperger's syndrome

      b. Carpel tunnel syndrome

      c. Trigger finger

      d. Raynaud's syndrome

Airborne concentrations of hydrocarbons are expressed in what unit of measure?

      a. STEL

      b. mg/m3

      c. kg/m2

      d. ppm

**The correct answer is (b)** A commonly reported problem associated with tingling, pain, or numbness in the thumb and first three fingers is referred to as carpel tunnel syndrome.

**The correct answer is (b)** Airborne concentrations of hydrocarbons are expressed in mg/m3 unit of measure.

What is the OSHA exposure limit for formaldehyde
based on an 8 hour TWA?

a. .82 ppm

b. .75 ppm

c. 1.0 ppm

d. 11 ppm

The quantity of radiation absorbed per unit mass is
a dose expressed in what?

a. microcuries

b. radioisotopes

c. minicuries

d. roentgens and rems

**The correct answer is (b)** The OSHA exposure limit for formaldehyde based on an 8 hour TWA is .75 ppm.

**The correct answer is (d)** The quantity of radiation absorbed per unit mass is a dose expressed in what roentgens and rems.

OSHA requires safety belt and lanyard hardware used in fall arrest systems to withstand a tensile load of how much in pounds?

    a. 4000

    b. 2000

    c. 3800

    d. 2200

An exposure monitoring and medical surveillance program must be in place for what level of ethylene oxide exposure?

    a. 2.0 ppm

    b. 1.0 ppm

    c. 0.5 ppm

    d. 0.025 ppm

**The correct answer is (a)** OSHA requires safety belt and lanyard hardware used in fall arrest systems to withstand a tensile load of 4000 pounds.

**The correct answer is (c)** An exposure monitoring and medical surveillance program must be in place for o.5 ppm level of ethylene oxide exposure.

**Hazardous Materials Spills may involve complex cleanup processes as well as OSHA and EPA reporting requirements. Which of the following choices below is NOT an action workers should take in their work area in response to a hazardous materials spill?**

a. Contact emergency personnel.

b. If exposed to a hazardous materials they should be instructed to remove contaminated
clothing immediately and be directed to the nearest safety shower or eye wash station.

c. Move injured victims from the immediate area if possible without further injury to
themselves or the victim.

d. Initiate clean-up of the hazardous material spill.

**Storage of Hazardous Materials is regulated by both EPA and OSHA regulations. Hazardous materials handling and storage has multiple implications for pollution prevention, storage, regulatory considerations, and facility management requirements. Which factor is not a factor the safety professional would consider a management issue for storage of hazardous materials?**

a. The use of proper control measures.

b. Determination of risks in storage.

c. Minimization of exposure.

d. Cost of replenishment.

**The correct answer is (d.)** Initiating clean-up of the hazardous material spill is NOT an action workers should take in their work area in response to a hazardous materials spill.

**The correct answer is (d.)** Storage of Hazardous Materials is regulated by both EPA and OSHA regulations. Hazardous materials handling and storage has multiple implications for pollution prevention, storage, regulatory considerations, and facility management requirements. The cost of replenishment is not a factor the safety professional would consider a management issue for storage of hazardous materials. They consider and establish a program based on the use of proper control measures, determine risks in storage, and controls to minimization exposure.

**Hypoxia is a condition in which the body as a whole or a local area of the body is deprived of adequate oxygen supply. Which industry may find employees which suffer from hypoxia?**

    a. Diving
    b. Coal mining
    c. Aviation
    d. Scaffold workers

**The safety professional will use the Product Life Cycle to determine the lifespan of an engineering control, PPE investment, or other safety purchase. There are four stages to the Product life cycle. Which of the following stage choices is NOT included in the product life cycle?**

    a. Introduction
    b. Growth
    c. Entrance
    d. Maturity

**The correct answer is (c.)** Hypoxia is a condition in which the body as a whole or a local area of the body is deprived of adequate oxygen supply. The aviation industry may find employees which suffer from hypoxia. hypoxia occurs in healthy people when they ascend to high altitude, where it causes altitude sickness leading to potentially fatal complications.

**The correct answer is (c.)** The safety professional will use the Product Life Cycle to determine the lifespan of an engineering control, PPE investment, or other safety purchase. The four stages to the Product life cycle are Introduction, Growth, Maturity, and Decline.

**In the safety field critical thinking skills provide the mental control and discipline required for situational assessment and decision making. Which of the following is NOT a skillset for critical thinking?**

a. Being aware of hazardous attitudes.
b. Being aware of all available resources
c. Effective planning, briefing and communication.
d. Not seeking feedback.

**The Occupational Safety and Health Agency (OSHA) was created by which ACT?**

a. The Occupational Safety and Health Act of 1970
b. The Occupational Safety Act of 1970
c. The Safety and Health Act of 1970
d. The Occupational Safety and Health Act of 1968

**The correct answer is (d.)** Not seeking feedback is NOT a skillset for critical thinking. The remaining choices are correct actions for critical thinking in the safety environment being aware of hazardous attitudes, being aware of all available resources, and effective planning, briefing and communication.

**The correct answer is (a.)** The Occupational Safety and Health Agency (OSHA) was created by the Occupational Safety and Health Act of 1970.

**Which of these choices is NOT included in the BCSP Code of Ethics?**
> a. BE honest, fair, and impartial; act with responsibility and integrity.
> b. ISSUE public statements only in an objective and truthful manner.
> c. UNDERTAKE All assignments asserting competence in the subject matter
> d. AVOID deceptive acts that falsify or misrepresent their academic or professional qualifications.

**The safety professional would use data extracted from the National Highway Traffic Safety Administration (NHTSA) for all of the following uses EXCEPT.**
> a. Recalls and defects
> b. Injury Vulnerability
> c. Crash Statistics
> d. Work related driver injuries

**The correct answer is (c.)** Of the choices UNDERTAKE All assignments asserting competence in the subject matter is not included in the Code of Ethics. The statement should read: UNDERTAKE assignments only when qualified by education or experience in the specific technical fields involved.

**The correct answer is (d.)** The safety professional would use data extracted from the National Highway Traffic Safety Administration (NHTSA) for all of the following, recalls and defects, injury vulnerability, and crash statistics EXCEPT work related driver injuries which would be retrieved from OSHA's website.

**Which of the following would a safety professional most likely search NIST data for?**
   a. Disaster and Failure Studies
   b. Cybersecurity questions
   c. Weather hazard analysis
   d. Chemical composition standards

**If an engineer in a chemical plant wanted to design a distillation column what process would best be suited for this?**
   a. Efficiency study
   b. Simulation
   c. Modeling
   d. 3-D Calculation

**The correct answer is (a.)** A safety professional would likely NIST data for data and failure studies. The NIST - National Institute of Standards and Technology is "a non-regulatory federal agency within the U.S. Department of Commerce whose mission is to promote U.S. innovation and industrial competitiveness by advancing measurement science, standards, and technology in ways that enhance economic security and improve our quality of life." NIST

**The correct answer is (b.)** If an engineer in a chemical plant wanted to design a distillation column a simulation would best be suited. The speed and accuracy of process simulation saves tremendous time and money particularly for design changes. The Certified Safety Professional will use or review safety simulations for safety processes.

Safety professionals can analyze trends and data from the Consumer Product Safety Commission (CPSC) which provides safety education, rules and laws, and research for injuries related to consumer products. Which of the following is a database by the CPSC with the total number of product-related injuries treated in hospital emergency rooms nationwide?

a. National Electronic Injury Surveillance System (NEISS)
b. Consumer Product Safety Commission (CPSC) Track
c. Consumer Watch (CPSCCW)
d. National Center for Safety (NCS)

Safety inspection goals are to maintain a safe work environment. If CSP Jamie were describing to their boss why safety inspections are used in departments which choice below would they NOT use as justification?

a. To comply with state and federal health and safety regulation.
b. To conduct target area inspections for areas which have a high potential for accidents.
c. To monitor problem employees.
d. To investigate a complaint of an unsafe or unhealthy situation.

**The correct answer is (a.)** Safety professionals can analyze trends and data from the Consumer Product Safety Commission (CPSC). The National Electronic Injury Surveillance System (NEISS) is a database by the CPSC with the total number of product-related injuries treated in hospital emergency rooms nationwide.

**The correct answer is (c.)** Safety inspection goals are to maintain a safe work environment. If CSP Jamie were describing to their boss why safety inspections are used in departments they would not use to monitor problem employees as justification.

On occasion the safety professional must provide expertise when there is disagreement in applicable safety procedures or in the development of documents as the subject matter expert in response to an accident or injury. Most often this expertise and documentation will be used for what?

a. Risk management proposals
b. Arbitration and mediation procedures
c. Survey analysis
d. FMEA

The diagram below shows a safety pyramid theory widely accepted for over 70 years and represents the theory of accident causation that unsafe acts lead to minor injuries and over time to major injuries. The theory is less accepted today. This is whose theory?

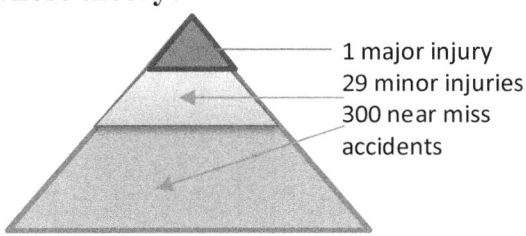

1 major injury
29 minor injuries
300 near miss accidents

a. Heinrich's
b. Goldblatt's
c. Reinich's
d. Brinert's

**The correct answer is (a.)** On occasion the safety professional must provide expertise when there is disagreement in applicable safety procedures or in the development of documents as the subject matter expert in response to an accident or injury. Most often this expertise and documentation will be used for arbitration and mediation procedures.

**The correct answer is (a.)** The diagram below shows a safety pyramid theory widely accepted for over 70 years and represents the theory of accident causation that unsafe acts lead to minor injuries and over time to major injuries. The pyramid proposes that for every 300 unsafe acts there are 29 minor injuries and one major injury. The theory is less accepted today. This is Heinrich's Pyramid Theory originated in 1931 by H.W. Heinrich.

**The scatter diagram is a graph that portrays the relationship between two continuous variables with the x-axis representing one variable and the y-axis representing the other. Safety professionals can use these diagrams to determine objectively whether a particular cause and effect are related. The diagram below shows what?**

a. Possible positive correlation
b. Positive correlation
c. Possible negative correlation
d. Negative correlation

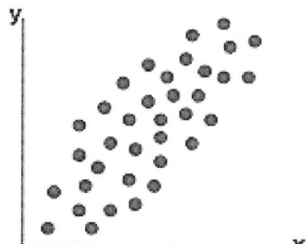

**Many companies consider safety, health, industrial hygiene, and environmental issues under the same auspice of safety management. Which of the following is an environmental problem a safety professional may be responsible for?**

    a. Fire, explosion and release of harmful substances into the environment.
    b. Reducing the organizations carbon footprint
    c. All of the above
    d. Regulatory compliance

**The correct answer is (a.)** The diagram shows possible positive correlation. If the variables are correlated the points will fall closely along a line or curve. The better the correlation the tighter the points will be to the line.

**The correct answer is (c.)** An environmental problem a safety professional may be responsible for may include fire, explosion and release of harmful substances into the environment, reducing the organizations carbon footprint, and regulatory compliance.

**Under the classes of hazardous materials infectious agents is classified under which category?**

    a. Hazard Class 2: Compressed Gases
    b. Hazard Class 6: Toxic Materials
    c. Hazard Class 9: Miscellaneous
    d. Hazard Class 5: Oxidizers and Organic Peroxides

**Under the category of job stress which of the following factors is not a contributor to a stressful work environment?**

    a. Inadequate resources to accomplish a task.
    b. Getting six to seven hours of uninterrupted sleep.
    c. Lack of input on job planning.
    d. Working in an unfamiliar area.

**The correct answer is (b.)** Under the classes of hazardous materials infectious agents is classified under Hazard Class 6: Toxic Materials.

**The correct answer is (b.)** Under the category of job stress getting six to seven hours of uninterrupted sleep is not a contributor to a stressful work environment.

**A safety professional has been asked to set as a member of a committee for organization risk management. Which will be the MOST important aspect they can provide as a member?**

a. Review of incidents
b. Making recommendations to prevent further loss
c. Implementing policy and procedures
d. Determining loss trends without financial information

**United States Code (USC) is the codification by subject matter of the general and permanent laws of the United States. It is divided by broad subjects into 51 titles and published by the Office of the Law Revision Counsel of the U.S. House of Representatives. Safety professionals will review Code of Federal Regulation (CFR) for laws and regulation for all of the following entities EXCEPT?**

a. Occupational Safety and Health Administration (OSHA)
b. American National Standards Institute – (ANSI)
c. Federal Emergency Management Agency (FEMA)
d. National Highway Traffic Safety Administration (NHTSA)

**The correct answer is (d.)** A safety professional has been asked to set as a member of a committee for organization risk management. Determining loss trends without financial information will be the MOST important aspect they can provide as a member because many companies mistakenly compare costs of prior year injuries to current year injuries.

**The correct answer is (b.)** Safety professionals will review Code of Federal Regulation (CFR) for laws and regulation for of the following entities except American National Standards Institute which is a voluntary organization not referenced by CFR regulations.

**A significant driver in workplace stress and psychological injuries is driven by interpersonal conflict between employees when issues are not resolved at an early stage. Which skillset would the safety professional use in a laboratory where a group of researchers had a significant number of altercations with another group?**

    a. Altercation reduction
    b. Conflict resolution
    c. Discipline and removal
    d. Advanced negotiation

**A safety professional is trying to determine a measure of correlation using ranks to calculate the correlation. Using this formula they are calculating the what?**

a. Spearman Correlation Coefficient

b. Newton's Law of Physics

$$r = 1 - \left( \frac{6 \sum d^2}{n(n^2 - 1)} \right)$$

c. William Haddon's Energy Theory

d. LEED Energy Consumption Rate

**The correct answer is (b.)** The safety professional would use conflict resolution in a laboratory where a group of researchers had a significant number of altercations with another group.

**The correct answer is (a.)** A safety professional is trying to determine a measure of correlation using ranks to calculate the correlation. Using this formula they are calculating the Spearman Correlation Coefficient which is a non-parametric measure of correlation using ranks to calculate the correlation.

$$r = 1 - \left( \frac{6 \sum d^2}{n(n^2 - 1)} \right)$$

**William Haddon's Energy Theory explains what?**

      a. Accidents are caused by energy out of control.

      b. Accidents are cause by management's lax attitudes towards safety.

      c. Accidents are directly proportional to unsafe behavior display.

      d. Accidents are 80% preventable

**A lung disease which occurs in two forms both simple and complicated, can be contracted by coal workers from breathing in dust from coal, graphite, or man-made carbon over a long period of time. This disease is called?**

      a. Pneumoconiosis

      b. Onomatopoeia

      c. COPD

      d. Rush's Disease

**The correct answer is (a.)** William Haddon's Energy Theory explains accidents are caused by energy out of control and that techniques can be used to reduce accidents, preventing the buildup of energy, reducing the initial amount of energy, preventing the release of energy, and controlling the release of energy.

**The correct answer is (a.)** A lung disease which occurs in two forms both simple and complicated, can be contracted by coal workers from breathing in dust from coal, graphite, or man-made carbon over a long period of time is called pneumoconiosis.

The CSP will need to be familiar with basic computer terminology and software applications which are necessary for safety program management and data manipulation. A software program that enables the computer hardware to communicate and operate with the computer software is the what?

a. Motherboard
b. Processor or CPU (Central Processing Unit)
c. Bios - (Basic Input/Output System)
d. Operating System (OS)

Ventilation is a method of controlling the environment with air flow. It is one of the most important engineering controls for improving or maintaining the quality of the air in the occupational work environment. Ventilation may be required in a confined space environment where the oxygen level is what?

a. (Oxygen is 19.5%–23.5%)
b. (Oxygen is 20.5%–22.5%)
c. (Oxygen is 22%–23.5%)
d. (Oxygen is 18%–18.5%)

**The correct answer is (d.)** The CSP will need to be familiar with basic computer terminology and software applications which are necessary for safety program management and data manipulation. A software program that enables the computer hardware to communicate and operate with the computer software is the Operating System (OS). The motherboard is the main circuit of the computer. The CPU is the brain of the computer. The BIOS is a program installed on the computer to start up the operating system.

**The correct answer is (d.)** Ventilation is a method of controlling the environment with air flow. It is one of the most important engineering controls for improving or maintaining the quality of the air in the occupational work environment. Ventilation may be required in a confined space environment where the oxygen level is less than 19.5% therefore d. is less than 19.5% at 18%–18.5%.

**Chemist William Henry is named for Henry's Law which is the principle that the amount of a gas dissolved at equilibrium in a given quantity of a liquid is proportional to the pressure of the gas in contact with the liquid. In the formula for Henry's Law $C=kP_{gas}$, the k is what?**

      a. k is Henry's law constant
      b. k is the partial pressure of the gas
      c. k is the solubility of a gas at a fixed temperature in a particular solvent
      d. k is an unknown variable

**The purpose of accident investigation is to determine procedural errors and hazards that contributed to the incident. Which of the following is NOT one of the three categories of causal factors?**

      a. Personal factors such as neglect of safety rules, lack of knowledge, or failure to understand procedure.
      b. Violation of procedures.
      c. Management force.
      d. Hazardous mechanical or physical conditions.

**The correct answer is (a.)** In the formula for Henry's Law C=kPgas, the k is Henry's law constant.

**The correct answer is (c.)** The purpose of accident investigation is to determine procedural errors and hazards that contributed to the incident. Management force is NOT one of the three categories of causal factors. The three causal factors are personal factors, violation of procedures, and management force.

**The CSP will primarily use internet research with the Department of Agriculture for?**

    a. Food safety and inspection information
    b. Pesticide and chemical safety
    c. Safety for the production of food sources
    d. Agricultural accident statistics.

**The safety professional may be subject to contract review for safety services. As such, they may be bound by privity. This means what?**

    a. A legal interpretation where both parties agree to keep interactions private.
    b. A legal interpretation in contract law where contracts are only binding on the parties
        signing the contract
    c. A legal interpretation where only one party is bound to the contract.
    d. A legal interpretation where in contract law both parties are subject to a privit time
        period.

**The correct answer is (a.)** The CSP will primarily use internet research with the Department of Agriculture for food safety and inspection information.

**The correct answer is (b.)** The safety professional may be subject to contract review for safety services. As such, they may be bound by privity. This a legal interpretation in contract law where contracts are only binding on the parties signing the contract.

The basic requirements for the control of documents is to have a procedures that includes a process to: keep track of revision numbers and that any changes made are identified, ensure that the latest versions of documents are available where they are to be used, ensure that documents are legible and identifiable, and identified and controlled. Which reference guides document control?

a. OSHA 1910
b. National Archives and Records Administration (NARA) 1204
c. OHSAS 18001
d. ISO 14000

Where would the safety professional be most likely to find administrative law published in the Federal Register by the executive departments and agencies of the federal government of the United States?

a. Federal Register Clauses
b. Code of Federal Regulations (CFR)
c. US Government Printing Office
d. US OPM

**The correct answer is (c.)** OHSAS 18001 guides document control. OHSAS is an international occupational health and safety management system specification for documentation.

**The correct answer is (d.)** The safety professional would be most likely to find administrative law published in the Federal Register by the executive departments and agencies of the federal government of the United States in the Code of Federal Regulations (CFR).

**The fault tree analysis (FTA) is a deductive analytical tool used to study a specific undesired event. The overall success of the FTA process depends on?**

    a. Statistical calculations
    b. Documentation of the process
    c. Sequence of events
    d. The skill of the analyst involved

**Safety professionals understand the effects of judgment and emotion in the interaction with employees. The phase of anger where an individual has reached a state where aggressive acts occur and unwillingness to comply occur can best be categorized as?**

    a. Rage
    b. Aggravation
    c. Anger
    d. Prevention

**The correct answer is (d.)** The fault tree analysis (FTA) is a deductive analytical tool used to study a specific undesired event. The overall success of the FTA process depends on the skill of the analyst involved.

**The correct answer is (b.)** The phase of anger where an individual has reached a state where aggressive acts occur and unwillingness to comply occur can best be categorized as rage.

**The Environmental Protection Agency (EPA) performs what two activities?**
- a. Compliance and enforcement
- b. Consultation and compliance
- c. Enforcement and audit
- d. Regulation and compliance

**In ergonomics a condition where the muscle to tendon junction becomes inflamed due to repeated abduction of a body part away from the body part to which it is attached is called ?**
- a. DeQuevain's disease
- b. Raynaud's Syndrome
- c. Trigger finger
- d. Tendinitis

**The correct answer is (a.)** The Environmental Protection Agency (EPA) performs compliance and enforcement.

**The correct answer is (d.)** In ergonomics a condition where the muscle to tendon junction becomes inflamed due to repeated abduction of a body part away from the body part to which it is attached is called tendinitis. DeQuervain's disease causes wrist deviation, Raynaud's Syndrome causes blood vessels to restrict with cold or vibration, and Trigger finger is caused by a finger being frequently flexed against resistance.

**Safety training and procedures typically involves coverage of four specific areas. Which of the following is NOT included?**
   a. Management commitment and planning
   b. Mitigation
   c. Hazard Correction and Control
   d. Hazard Assessment

**Which of the following choices is NOT a characteristic of a confined space?**
   a. Has the potential to contain a hazardous atmosphere.
   b. Has an internal configuration that could trap or asphyxiate an entrant.
   c. Contains a material that can engulf an entrant.
   d. Contains no light source.

**The correct answer is (b.)** Safety training and procedures typically involves coverage of four specific areas. Management commitment and planning, hazard correction and control, hazard assessment, and safety and health training. Not mitigation.

**The correct answer is (d.)** Contains not light source is NOT a characteristic of a confined space. Confined spaces may have adequate lighting.

**The act of reviewing accident reports, inspections from regulatory agencies, insurance companies and material safety data sheets or sds would be the performance of what?**

   a. A safety audit
   b. A safety presentation
   c. A safety class
   d. A safety review

**If a safety professional wanted to show how a process changes over time with data plotted in time order. The best display of this data would be?**

   a. Control Chart
   b. Pie chart
   c. Gantt Chart
   d. Scatter diagram

**The correct answer is (c.)** The act of reviewing accident reports, inspections from regulatory agencies, insurance companies and material safety data sheets or sds would be the performance of what a safety audit.

**The correct answer is (a.)** If a safety professional wanted to show how a process changes over time with data plotted in time order. The best display of this data would be a control chart.

**Which of the following would NOT be a deficient attribute in a safety climate survey?**
   a. Lessons learned disregarded
   b. Little preparation for emergency events
   c. Respect for the limitation of technology
   d. Invincible mindset

**Which of the following would NOT be a positive attribute in a safety climate survey?**
   a. Maximizing safety design
   b. Teamwork practices are encouraged
   c. Clear accountability
   d. Compliance means safe enough

**The correct answer is (c.)** Respect for the limitation of technology would NOT be a deficient attribute in a safety climate survey. It would be a positive attribute.

**The correct answer is (d.)** Compliance means safe enough would NOT be a positive attribute in a safety climate survey. It would be a deficient attribute simple compliance does not improve performance.

**The Occupational Health and Safety Management System (OHSMS) requires written methods for all of the following EXCEPT?**
  a. Research of engineering controls
  b. Conducting risk assessments
  c. Performing hazard analysis
  d. Training employees

**The safety professional is responsible to implement a system to plan for designing, measuring, evaluating and improving key safety processes and increase performance. This process is called?**
  a. Contemplation system
  b. Evaluation system
  c. Batched profile
  d. Safety Process Management

**The correct answer is (a.)** The Occupational Health and Safety Management System (OHSMS) requires written methods for all of the following EXCEPT research of engineering controls. This is not required as a written method.

**The correct answer is (b.)** The safety professional is responsible to implement a system to plan for designing, measuring, evaluating and improving key safety processes and increase performance. This process is called the evaluation system.

**Which of the following attributes is NOT associated with an exit?**

    a. Must be opened without keys or tools.
    b. Must lead to a safe area.
    c. Must lead to the exterior.
    d. Must be marked with an "exit" sign.

**The BCSP has a Professional Conduct set of standards this requires the following. Which one is incorrect?**

a. Hold paramount the safety and health of people, the protection of the environment and
    protection of property in the performance of professional duties.
b. Issue public statements only in an objective and truthful manner.
c. Seeking opportunities to be of constructive service in civic affairs is not required.
d. Undertake assignments only when qualified by education or experience in the specific
    technical fields involved.

**The correct answer is (c.)** The attribute NOT associated with an exit is, "must lead to the exterior". This is not required as long as the exit leads to a safe area.

**The correct answer is (c.)** The BCSP has a Professional Conduct set of standards this requires the following. Seeking opportunities to be of constructive service in civic affairs is not required, is an incorrect response. CSP's should seek civic opportunities to advance the profession.

**Using Safety Software Modules to generate an OSHA 301 report and 300 log and track the investigation, analysis, and documentation of occupational accidents and illnesses would most likely help with a review of safety what?**

      a. Population demographics
      b. Accident causes
      c. Time of day
      d. Investigation stubs

**Which of the following would NOT be a consideration for the multiple factor theory in an example where a factory worker is in a hurry and walks through a dimly lit warehouse and trips over a wheel chock?**

      a. If the worker were on vacation they would not have tripped on the wheel chock?
      b. If the worker was not in a hurry and were more aware of their surroundings would they
            have avoided the wheel chock?
      c. Was it necessary for the worker to walk in that area or was there a more safe route?
      d. If the area were better lit would the worker have avoided the wheel chock?

**The correct answer is (a.)** Using Safety Software Modules to generate an OSHA 301 report and 300 log and track the investigation, analysis, and documentation of occupational accidents and illnesses would most likely help with a review of safety population demographics. Accident causes and time of day are a subset of population demographics.

**The correct answer is** (a.) If the worker were on vacation they would not have tripped on the wheel chock would NOT be a consideration for the multiple factor theory in an example where a factory worker is in a hurry and walks through a dimly lit warehouse and trips over a wheel chock because vacation time is an independent variable from the causes described.

**During a fire activation, employees did not know emergency exit routes. This is required under initial assignment and required in the emergency action plan under what?**

    a. OSHA 1910.39
    b. NFPA 101
    c. HAZCOM
    d. HAZWOPER

**The mission of The National Institute for Occupational Safety and Health (NIOSH) NIOSH in terms of safety is?**

    a. To provide epidemiology training.
    b. To provide leadership for the prevention of injury and illness among workers who must rely on personal protective equipment.
    c. To preserve the public's safety and health when disasters strike.
    d. To provide practical solutions vital to reducing risks of injury and death in traditional industries.

**The correct answer is (a.)** During a fire activation, employees did not know emergency exit routes. This is required under initial assignment and required in the emergency action plan under what OSHA 1910.39.

**The correct answer is (a.)** The mission of The National Institute for Occupational Safety and Health (NIOSH) in terms of safety is to provide practical solutions vital to reducing risks of injury and death in traditional industries.

**Anthropometry is used in occupational injury prevention to evaluate the interaction of workers with tasks, tools, machines, vehicles, and personal protective equipment. What is anthropometry?**

   a. A measurement system used to determine force and weight.
   b. The science that defines physical measures of a person's size, form, and functional
         capacities.
   c. A form of ergonomic measure.
   d. A measurement software.

**Understanding safety motivation theories helps the safety professional to understand worker conduct and action for work safety. A common safety motivation theory is Maslow's hierarchy of need. Maslow's theory includes 5 need categories which include safety, self-actualization and three of the following. Which choice is NOT included in one of the five categories?**

   a. Esteem
   b. Physiological
   c. Financial
   d. Belongingness

**The correct answer is (b.)** Anthropometry is used in occupational injury prevention to evaluate the interaction of workers with tasks, tools, machines, vehicles, and personal protective equipment. Anthropometry is the science that defines physical measures of a person's size, form, and functional capacities.

**The correct answer is (c.)** Maslow's theory includes 5 need categories which include safety, self-actualization, esteem, physiological, and belongingness. Financial is NOT included in one of the five categories.

**Safety professionals may review structural and dynamic failure test results. A tensile test is a fundamental type of mechanical test that can be performed on material to determine its mechanical properties. Based on the total strain that a material undergoes before breaking into two pieces, ductile materials are those that undergo what?**

a. Larger strain (more than 5%) before breakage
b. Breaks before any appreciable strain (less than 5%)
c. Smaller strain (more than 95%) before breakage
d. Breaks before any appreciable strain (less than 95%)

**The Pythagorean Theorem is used to calculate?**

a. The third side of a triangle if two sides are known.
b. The weight of a Pythagorean wedge.
c. The wavelength of a light wave.
d. Gas weight in a cylinder.

**The correct answer is (a.)** Ductile materials are those that undergo larger strain (more than 5%) before breakage.

**The correct answer is (a.)** The Pythagorean Theorem is used to calculate the third side of a triangle if two sides are known.

The mission of the National Fire Protection Association (NFPA) is to reduce the worldwide burden of fire and other hazards on the quality of life. Which of the following is NOT provided by the NFPA?

    a. Research
    b. Consensus codes and standards
    c. Training
    d. Enforcement

A Job Safety Analysis (JAS) typically involves identification of tasks or equipment that should be modified to reduce human exposure. Additionally a JAS involves all of the following steps EXCEPT?

    a. Identification of hazards that developed as a result of a task.
    b. Physical conditioning documentation.
    c. Break down a job into the sequence of tasks.
    d. Review environmental conditions.

**The correct answer is (d.)** The mission of the National Fire Protection Association (NFPA) is to reduce the worldwide burden of fire and other hazards on the quality of life. Enforcement is not provided by the NFPA.

**The correct answer is (b.)** A Job Safety Analysis (JAS) typically involves identification of tasks or equipment that should be modified to reduce human exposure. Additionally a JAS involves all of the following steps EXCEPT physical conditioning documentation. This would typically not be available or tangible to job safety.

Toxicity is defined as a hazardous material that has the ability to cause illness or death in man, animals, fish, or plants. Toxicity of exposure is affected by three factors, length of exposure, toxicity of a hazardous substance, and what?

a. Individual susceptibility
b. Permissible exposure limit
c. Concentration per mg/kg
d. Temperature

OSHA's blood borne pathogen standard requires the employer to prepare a written exposure control plan. If the employer's jobs have the potential for exposure to blood borne pathogens they must include training. Which of the following is NOT a required training element?

a. Procedures to follow if exposure occurs.
b. Effectiveness of platelet antidotes.
c. Recognition of tasks that may involve exposure.
d. Explanations of the modes of transmission

**The correct answer is (d.)** Toxicity is defined as a hazardous material that has the ability to cause illness or death in man, animals, fish, or plants. Toxicity of exposure is affected by three factors, length of exposure, toxicity of a hazardous substance, and what individual susceptibility.

**The correct answer is (b.)** If the employer's jobs have the potential for exposure to blood borne pathogens they must include training. Effectiveness of platelet antidotes is NOT a required training element and incorrect. The training should include the effectiveness of the hepatitis B vaccine.

**Prevention of tripping hazards is a requirement for safety professionals. Which of the following choices is NOT a preventative measure for tripping hazards?**

a. Ensure areas are well lit.
b. Ensure work areas are kept clean and materials in appropriate storage.
c. Properly maintain walking area maintenance related hazards.
d. Build mechanical means of travel.

**A health hazard is a chemical for which significant evidence based studies exist to show that acute or chronic health effects may occur with exposure. Which of the following is NOT a type of health hazard?**
a. Teratogenic
b. Mutagenic
c. Corrosive
d. Flammable

**The correct answer is (d.)** Building mechanical means of travel is not a preventative measure for tripping hazards as a preventative step.

**The correct answer is (d.)** Flammable is NOT a type of health hazard it is a type of atmospheric hazard.

**Bureau of Labor Statistics (BLS) Wage Data by area and occupation help the safety professional to calculate.**
   a. Injury rates per thousand
   b. Injury rates per population
   c. Injury rates per industry
   d. Injury rates of elderly

**As a CSP your HAZCOM program must include all of the following EXCEPT?**
   a. Training on chemical safety in the workplace
   b. Available MSDS or SDS
   c. Written Communication Plan
   d. Active compliance monitoring by computer software

**The correct answer is (c.)** Bureau of Labor Statistics (BLS) Wage Data by area and occupation help the safety professional to calculate injury rates per industry.

**The correct answer is (d.)** As a CSP your HAZCOM program must include all of the following EXCEPT active compliance monitoring by computer software.

A crew of concrete workers is pouring roadways in an excessive heat warning. One of the workers experiences a heat related disorder. During the episode the worker was mentally confused and had convulsions. Which type of disorder was he most likely to have had?

a. Heat cramps
b. Fatigue
c. Heat exhaustion
d. Heat stroke

The facility development process is a project management application which contains the steps of a project for all phases. Which type of application is the facility development process most commonly used?

a. Reengineering of a safety accident
b. Design and build of a facility
c. Development of a strategic plan
d. Process improvement

**The correct answer is (d.)** The mental confusion and convulsions symptoms most likely were the result of heat stroke.

**The correct answer is (b.)** The facility development process is most commonly used in the design and build of a facility from project recognition, needs assessment, go—no go, design, bidding, construction, and occupancy.

**A safety professional is training employees with a supervisor for the proper transfer of flammable solvents. Which of these pieces of equipment would not be used in the training?**

    a. Transfer pump
    b. A hygrometer
    c. A bonding wire
    d. Non sparking bung wrench

**Which of the following is NOT a requirement in a workplace with lead exposure higher than the PEL limit?**

    a. Medical monitoring program
    b. Warning signs in areas higher than the PEL
    c. Pb recycling
    d. PPE provision

**The correct answer is (b.)** A safety professional training employees with a supervisor for the proper transfer of flammable solvents would not use a hygrometer. A hygrometer is an instrument used for measuring the moisture content in the environment not a factor during transfer.

**The correct answer is (c.)** A medical monitoring program, warning signs in areas higher than the PEL, and PPR provision are required. Recycling the lead is not required but may be incorporated into the facilities environmental programs.

**Department of Health and Human Services is the United States government's principal agency for protecting the health of all Americans and providing essential human services. The safety professional will most often use the HHS website to?**

      a. Determine worker compensation rates.
      b. Determine healthcare costs related to accidents and injury.
      c. Determine geographic injury rates.
      d. Determine ICD9's

**Noise is measured in frequency (pitch) and intensity (decibels) which type of noise would a manufacturing engine be classified?**

      a. Impulse
      b. Narrow band
      c. Wide band
      d. Constant

**The correct answer is (b.)** Department of Health and Human Services is the United States government's principal agency for protecting the health of all Americans and providing essential human services. The safety professional will most often use the HHS website to determine healthcare costs related to accidents and injury.

**The correct answer is (c.)** Noise is measured in frequency (pitch) and intensity (decibels) and a manufacturing engine would be classified as wide band. Narrow band examples would include hand power tools, impulse would include a jack hammer, and constant is not a type of noise.

**Dalton's Law of Partial Pressures**

$$P_T = P_1 + P_2 + P_3 + \ldots$$

**is most often used by safety professionals to calculate?**

    a. The constant pressure of a gas relative to atmospheric pressure.

    b. The total pressure of gas in a line.

    c. The individual pressures of each gas in a mixture of gases.

    d. The total chemical composition of a gaseous formula.

**Machine safeguarding reduces the risk of injury through guards, devises, distance, or automated feeding of material. Which type of machine guarding is most appropriate for mechanical power presses?**

    a. Restraint

    b. Pullback

    c. Gate

    d. Sensing

**The correct answer is (c.)** Dalton's Law of Partial Pressures is most often used by safety professionals to calculate the individual pressures of each gas in a mixture of gases.

**The correct answer is (a.)** A restraint type of machine guarding is most appropriate for mechanical power presses. Sometimes referred to as holdouts they are appropriate safeguards for both full and part revolution mechanical power presses.

A safety professional is communicating safety information using American National Standards Institute (ANSI) communication schemes. A sign for general safety instructions would be placed on what type of background?

    a. Green
    b. Orange
    c. Blue
    d. Yellow

Ohm's Law is most often represented by which formula?

    a. $V=IR$
    b. $P=VI$
    c. $R=\rho A$
    d.
       $R=\rho\dfrac{L}{A}$

**The correct answer is (b.).** A sign for general safety instructions would be placed on a green safety sign. OSHA specifies that the standard color for safety instruction signs shall be a white background, green panel and white letters

**The correct answer is (a.).** Ohm's Law is most often represented by V=IR. Ohm's Law is given by: $V = I R$. where V is the potential difference between two points which include a resistance R.

**The function of Federal Emergency Management Agency (FEMA) is to what?**

    a. Develop Mitigation plans.

    b. Respond to emergency events upon activation of the President.

    c. Provide disaster assistance to state governments.

    d. Support citizens and first responders to ensure capability to prepare for, protect against, respond to, recover from and mitigate all hazards.

**OSHA estimates there are approximately 1.5 million forklifts in the US. Which of the following is not included in common operator errors?**

    a. Tipovers

    b. Hydraulic failure

    c. Falling from a platform held by a forklift

    d. Being crushed between

**The correct answer is (d.)** The function of the Federal Emergency Management Agency is to support citizens and first responders to ensure capability to prepare for, protect against, respond to, recover from and mitigate all hazards.

**The correct answer is (b.)** Hydraulic failure is not included in common operator errors. Hydraulic failure is a form of mechanical failure.

Elise is a safety professional performing a chi-square analysis of the data found to have significant influence on the computed physical, emotional, and intellectual of workers in her manufacturing facility in attempt to prevent accident occurrence. She is identifying the consistent recurring day cycles tied to biorhythms so that the workers could be kept away from the hazardous tasks on critical days. These days include all of the following cycles EXCEPT?

a. 20
b. 23
c. 28
d. 33

The flashpoint is the temperature where a liquid produces enough vapor to ignite. A flammable liquid that has a flashpoint below 73 degrees and having a boiling point above 100 degrees is what class?

a. Class 1
b. Class 1A
c. Class 1B
d. Class 1C

**The correct answer is (a).** Biorhythm theory postulates that variations in human abilities are governed by three consistently recurring cycles of 23, 28, and 33 days length. 20 days is not a recurring cycle.

**The correct answer is (c.)** A flammable liquid that has a flashpoint below 73 degrees and having a boiling point above 100 degrees is Class 1B. Class 1 has closed cup flash points below 100 degrees Fahrenheit and having vapor pressures not exceeding 40 psi. Class 1A has a flashpoint below 73 degrees and having a boiling point below 100 degrees. Class 1C has flash points at or above 73 degrees and below 100 degrees Fahrenheit.

**Which of the following is the correct listing of the elements of process safety management included process hazard analysis?**

a. Identification, evaluation, analysis, previous incidents, engineering, and administrative controls.

b. Identification, evaluation, control of process hazards, previous incidents, engineering, and administrative controls.

c. Identification, evaluation, engineering, and administrative controls.

d. Control of process hazards, previous incidents, engineering, and administrative controls.

**The psychometric chart is used in safety management for what application?**

a. Tensile strength
b. Ergonomics
c. Heat Stress and relative humidity
d Tongue weight

**The correct answer is (b.)** Identification, evaluation, control of process hazards, previous incidents, engineering, and administrative controls is the correct listing of the elements of process safety management included process hazard analysis.

**The correct answer is (c.)** The psychometric chart is used in safety management for
heat stress and relative humidity determinations.

**A safety professional determining respirator selection for cleaning of an indoor chemical storage tank would consider all of the following EXCEPT?**

      a. Toxicity of the contaminants
      b. Oxygen presence
      c. Concentration in the air
      d. Chemical flashpoint

**Which of the following is NOT an application for atmosphere supplying respirators?**

      a. Contaminant concentrations are immediately dangerous to life and health (IDLH)
      b. Insufficient oxygen
      c. Unknown contaminant concentration
      d. 20.8 to 21 percent oxygen concentration

**The correct answer is (d.)** A safety professional determining respirator selection for cleaning of an indoor chemical storage tank would consider all of the following EXCEPT chemical flashpoint. Flashpoint is not a consideration in respirator selection it would be a consideration for cleaning the storage tank.

**The correct answer is (d.)** 0.8 to 21 percent oxygen concentration is normal range and is NOT an application for atmosphere supplying respirators.